THE FABER LIBRARY

OF ILLUMINATED MANUSCRIPTS

edited by Walter Oakeshott

The

Parisian Miniaturist

Honoré

THE FABER LIBRARY OF ILLUMINATED MANUSCRIPTS

edited by Walter Oakeshott

THE BENEDICTIONAL OF ST. ETHELWOLD
Francis Wormald

THE PARISIAN MINIATURIST HONORÉ
Eric G. Millar

THE GREAT LAMBETH BIBLE
C. R. Dodwell

THE ROHAN BOOK OF HOURS
Jean Porcher

THE VIENNA GENESIS
E. Wellesz

A FIFTEENTH CENTURY PLUTARCH
Charles Mitchell

THE
PARISIAN MINIATURIST
HONORÉ

with an introduction and notes

by

ERIC G. MILLAR

FABER AND FABER LIMITED

24 Russell Square London

FIRST PUBLISHED IN MCMLIX
BY FABER AND FABER LIMITED
24 RUSSELL SQUARE LONDON WC I
PRINTED IN GREAT BRITAIN
BY WESTERN PRINTING SERVICES LTD., BRISTOL
COLOUR PLATES MADE AND PRINTED
BY FINE ART ENGRAVERS LTD., GUILDFORD
ALL RIGHTS RESERVED

© 1959 BY FABER AND FABER LIMITED

To

SYDNEY COCKERELL

1. General Introduction

'*Thirteenth Century*—This is commonly regarded as the greatest of all in medieval history; and truly, when we think of achievements such as Westminster, Amiens, and Chartres, and of men such as St. Louis, St. Thomas Aquinas, St. Francis, Dante, Edward I, Roger Bacon, we must agree that the popular estimate is sound. Certainly we see in France and in England the fine flower of art in buildings and in books.

Paris is still the centre. The "Gothic" spirit is concentrated there. The book trade is enormous. It is passing—under the influence of the University, most likely—out of the hands of the monastic scribes into those of the professional "stationers"; while great individual artists, such as Honoré, arise to provide for Royal and noble persons examples of art which stand as high to-day as when they were first produced.'

M. R. JAMES, *The Wanderings and Homes of Manuscripts*, 1919.

No better or more concise survey of the period can be imagined than this quotation from a small book which it is safe to say that only the late Dr. James could have written. The thirteenth century was indeed the supreme period of the middle ages so far as the arts are concerned. Every century of course had its great creative artists and craftsmen and its outstanding masterpieces, but in this century, of all others, architects, sculptors, workers in stained glass, painters and illuminators, and craftsmen of all kinds seem to have been animated by a burning desire to produce only what was of the greatest beauty and perfection, and the general level attained throughout was astonishingly high. Nowhere is this more evident than in the lovely illuminated manuscripts of the period, the best of which have never been surpassed, if they have even been equalled, in any age. John Ruskin once wrote:— 'I can't conceive anybody being ever tried with a heavier temptation than I am to save every farthing I can to collect a rich shelf of thirteenth century manuscripts', a sentence which the late Mr. Yates Thompson reprinted in appreciation as a heading to one of the volumes of the Catalogue of his own famous collection.

And, very fortunately, illuminated manuscripts have survived in large quantities, in spite of all the destruction that has gone on since medieval times and into the nineteenth century, in which latter period, especially, some misguided persons had a liking for cutting out the miniatures and pasting them into scrap-books. Even Ruskin himself, despite the sentiments quoted above, thought nothing of dismembering some of his manuscripts, and his best ones at that, and distributing detached leaves to favoured friends and institutions, always, no doubt, with the highest motives. Nor can one forget the two world wars of the present century, in the first of which at least one masterpiece, the magnificent fourteenth-century English Psalter at Douai, was totally ruined by damp owing to its having been buried by the Librarian when it might have been removed to a place of safety. The losses due to the last war are probably not yet fully known, but I was distressed to learn only a few months ago that the Library of Chartres, with its many fine manuscripts, was a total loss through bombing.

Quite apart from the great beauty of the finest examples, illuminated manuscripts are our chief authority for the costumes, armour, and other accessories of their time, for there were no such persons as antiquaries in the middle ages, and Biblical and other personages were always represented in the costumes of the country and period of the manuscripts themselves. It is to illuminated manuscripts, therefore, that we must turn, not only for these details, but also for much of our knowledge of daily life in the middle ages, for, very fortunately, although the large majority of these books were of a religious character, the conventions, at least by the middle of the thirteenth century, did not exclude the introduction of secular subjects in the margins and elsewhere. (The delightful hunting scene reproduced in Plate 4 is an example, having no connection whatever with the subject of the miniature or with any part of the text.) Their importance was not perhaps generally recognized even as comparatively recently as 1908, when Sir Sydney Cockerell could write in his preface to the Catalogue of the splendid exhibition held in that year at the Burlington Fine Arts Club:—'It is obvious that painted books which have not suffered from wanton damage or neglect are practically as they left the artists' hands, many centuries ago. The colours are as vivid as ever, the lines as sharp, and the brush of the restorer has not reached them. Nevertheless, professed students of art, with a few notable exceptions, have chosen to regard them as interesting toys, quite outside the scope of their more serious investigations.' The position, however, has changed since then, as is shown, if in no other way, by the prices commanded by the finer examples on the increasingly rare occasions when they come into the sale room, and are eagerly sought after by the great libraries and private collectors. Much is also being done to stimulate interest by the publication of reproductions of all kinds.

In many people's minds there is the idea that illuminated manuscripts were produced only in the monasteries, and this is no doubt true as regards the earlier periods, let us say until the end of the twelfth century. Even so, it is difficult to speak with any certainty; how far, for example, did artists go from one religious house to another to carry out some special piece of work, and were these artists ever laymen, even in the earlier periods? In England, to take only one example, the same artist, or an artist working in precisely the same style, would seem to have had a hand in some manuscripts executed in the first half of the twelfth century for both St. Alban's Abbey and the Abbey of Bury St. Edmunds, and we do not know at present whether he was a monk lent by one Abbey to the other, or whether he was an independent person, monk or layman, coming from some centre outside and executing commissions as required. There is at least no doubt that by the thirteenth century a number of lay ateliers were coming into existence and carrying out work for Royal and other patrons, as already indicated in the quotation from Dr. James's book, and although manuscripts of the highest quality no doubt continued to be produced simultaneously in the scriptoria of the great Abbeys, this work was no longer a monopoly of the Religious Houses.

It is indeed tantalizing that, with so much material surviving, so little is really known of the makers of these books or of the conditions under which the books were made, and we have to depend almost entirely on conjecture. A question invariably asked by casual visitors to the British Museum, after ascertaining that a given manuscript was written by hand and that real gold was used, was how long it took to make it, a transatlantic gentleman even going so far as to say of a particularly beautiful and delicate miniature that I was showing him, 'That's real fine; that's what we call the State Prison Touch out there', and to reply, on being asked for an explanation, that he reckoned that no one who was not in the State Prison could have the time to do it! But the answer, of course, is that one does not know. Much must have depended, for one thing, on the number of persons employed on any particular manuscript, which must have varied considerably. One would especially like to know the procedure in the case of the miraculous little portable Bibles, of which one could almost say that there was a kind of mass production, especially in Paris, in the second half of the thirteenth century. Quantities of these are to be found still in all the great Libraries, and in most private collections, for until recently they were hardly less common in the market than fifteenth-century Books of Hours. The writing of the text is of almost incredible minuteness—the late Professor Middleton owned one of these Bibles written throughout on a scale of fifteen lines to the inch—and any one of these books would have taken a lifetime to execute, or so one would have imagined, quite apart from the strain on the eyesight of both the scribe and the illuminator, for many of these have initials with tiny pictures to scale. The vellum used for these little books is of extraordinary thinness combined with perfect opacity; the secret of its manufacture is entirely lost.

The production of an important manuscript must certainly have been the work of several persons. Its planning, at least so far as the decoration is concerned, was no doubt carried out by one man, presumably the head of the atelier, and it is not uncommon to find evidence of this in written instructions or even sketches in plummet (the medieval lead pencil) in the margins, where the latter have not been too badly trimmed by the binders. A thirteenth century Bible in my own collection, executed in the neighbourhood of York, has a number of these instructions in Latin, such as 'Balaam sitting on the ass and the angel', 'David, an old man, crowned, seated on throne. A girl standing below',' a prophet sitting and weeping below, and a city above', these instructions being duly carried out in the initials. The scribe or scribes, for there were usually more than one, wrote the text, leaving blank spaces for the rubricators, (that is to say the writers of the passages in red ink, chapter headings, and so on, who were no doubt in some cases the scribes themselves) and for the persons executing the red and blue flourished and penwork initials. Spaces were of course left also for the illuminators, whether these were decorators or figure-draughtsmen or both; the former would be responsible for the ornamental initials and borders only, leaving the more important work to the figure draughtsmen, but some of the latter, especially the head of the atelier, may have carried out all the ornamental work on a given page in special cases. All these persons must normally have worked together in a more or less uniform style, and as a general rule it is extremely difficult to distinguish them apart, especially as we do not even know how far one artist may have carried out the drawings and handed out some of them to other artists to colour. The head of the atelier may also have put finishing touches to other artists' work.

The same compositions often occur in two or more manuscripts, and in such cases it is usually safe to assume that the manuscripts in question were executed in the same atelier. It sometimes happens, however, that the compositions in one manuscript may reappear in another of later date and in a different style, in which case the later manuscript may well have been copied from the earlier one in some quite different centre, for most manuscripts are easily portable.

We should know even less than we actually do of the methods employed in their production, were it not that one or two important books have been left unfinished and show the different stages of their execution. The great twelfth-century Bible in Winchester Cathedral Library is one of these; another is the lovely thirteenth-century Apocalypse, MS. Douce 180 in the Bodleian Library. An even better example is the early fourteenth-century Metz Pontifical, now in the Fitzwilliam Museum, Cambridge, by the gift of the late Mr. Yates Thompson, to whom it had been bequeathed by his friend and fellow collector, Sir Thomas Brooke. Sir Sydney Cockerell, who was Director of the Fitzwilliam Museum at the time of its acquisition, was able to make a close study of this very beautiful manuscript, which he has described as 'perhaps the most instructive of the numerous manuscripts that have come down to us unfinished', and has written as follows of the process of completion as revealed by it:— 'First the pictures were beautifully drawn in outline, then this outline was all but obliterated by a thin coat of white pigment covering the whole of the area, then came the gilding and burnishing, then the colouring, and finally the repetition, more or less exactly, of the original outline.'

As regards the gilding, two kinds of gold were employed, burnished and matt, the gold for the latter being ground down and used as a pigment. For the former, actual gold leaf was used, beaten down to the required degree of thinness and laid on the page after the ground had been prepared and built up with gesso; it was then burnished with an agate. It is this burnished gold that still defies even the most modern methods of reproduction, and even when real gold is used it is almost impossible to give the effect of the original, while in any case the cost is prohibitive; in my own experience in the nineteen twenties, the gold for a particular plate cost £20 as against five shillings if bronze had been used instead. Bronze is anyhow unsatisfactory, as it soon turns black, and in most cases, as in the present publication, yellow is the best compromise.

For some reason that has never been really explained, the medieval illuminator seems to have been regarded, or at least to have regarded himself, as a person altogether inferior to the scribe. It is thus by no means unusual to find the name of the latter set out in a colophon at the end of a manuscript, occasionally with elaborate details, as in a fine late twelfth-century Bible at Paris, the writer of which, a scribe from Canterbury named Manerius, has given full particulars of himself and his parentage, with some highly uncomplimentary remarks about his various relatives. The illuminators, on the other hand, even the greatest of them, and many of them were great artists in every sense of the word, seem to have been content to remain anonymous, and it is often only from chance entries in contemporary documents that even their names have come down to us, as for example in an Oxford deed of about 1180, in which three of the witnesses are illuminators named Peter, Ralph and William. But we are as far as ever from identifying any of their work. Cases of illuminators signing their work are of the utmost rarity. A late eleventh-century manuscript in Durham Cathedral Library supplies one example in a signed portrait of a monk Robert Benjamin, who painted the initials for Bishop Carilef. I can think of two in the twelfth century, the first of whom, Hugh the painter, has

8

put his name 'Hugo Pictor' to a small portrait in a manuscript in the Bodleian Library, Bodley 717, with a further note saying he was the painter and illuminator of the work. This manuscript, which was executed about the year 1100, belonged to Exeter Cathedral but was probably produced in Normandy. The other example, so far as I know, is unique, as it is a case of a woman, whose portrait of herself as a nun occurs in a manuscript at Frankfort, with the inscription 'Guda, a sinner, a woman, wrote and painted this book', showing her to have been the scribe as well. There are a few instances in the thirteenth century. I only know of one in England, W. de Brailes, working probably in Oxford about 1240, who is well known through the discoveries and researches of Sir Sydney Cockerell. Two of his productions are

Note (enlarged) giving the names of two scribes and an illuminator, from a manuscript executed in N.E. France about A.D. 1280, in the collection of the author.

[" . . . Me scripsit Johannes dictus Campions et Arnulphus de camphaing. Et Gossuins de lecaucie lenlumina." (*John called Campions and Arnold de Camphaing wrote me And Gossvins de lecaucie illuminated it.*)]

signed by him, and as he worked in a distinctive style, rather peculiarly his own, it has been possible to recognize four others which do not contain his name. Two French examples are known to me, the first somewhat intimately, as it is in my own collection, by the generous gift of Sir Sydney Cockerell, to whom it belonged for more than half a century. This is a small volume containing extracts from the works of St. Augustine and a work of St. John of Damascus, beautifully written and decorated with six fine initials, about the year 1280, and containing a note in red, in Latin, stating that it was written by John called Campions and Arnold de Camphaing, to which is added a line in blue ink, in a different hand and in French, 'and Gossvins de lecaucie illuminated it'. As Sir Sydney himself wrote of it, 'very few books of this period exist in which the names of both scribes and illuminator are given'. The other example is a volume of Lives of Saints, Franç. 412 in the Bibliothèque Nationale

B   9 at Paris, which is dated 1285 and contains a note giving the illuminator's name as Henry. Others no doubt exist, but I do not know of any myself.

Until the early part of the thirteenth century, England may be said to have taken the lead in the production of illuminated manuscripts. There are, for example, no continental rivals to the pre-Conquest Winchester school, the supreme example of which, the well-known Benedictional of St. Ethelwold, has recently been acquired by the British Museum. Nor can anything executed abroad in the twelfth century stand comparison with the great English Bibles of the period, such as the Bury St. Edmunds Bible at Corpus Christi College, Cambridge, or the Winchester Bible, already mentioned in another connection, or with the York Psalters at Glasgow and Copenhagen respectively. The marvellous Psalter of Queen Ingeburge of Denmark, now in the Musée Condé at Chantilly, seems to have been executed in France, probably before 1214, but it shows the strongest English influence and may even have been the work of English artists who crossed the channel. France, again, had nothing finer to show than the two Peterborough Psalters of about the year 1220, now belonging respectively to the Society of Antiquaries of London and the Fitzwilliam Museum, Cambridge.

The accession, however, of St. Louis in 1226 completely changed the picture and brought Paris into the forefront, a position which it continued to occupy for the rest of the middle ages, and during his long reign a series of incomparable manuscripts was produced, of which Sir Sydney Cockerell has so aptly written that they were 'treasures worthy to have the Sainte Chapelle for a casket'. One need only think in this connection of St. Louis's own exquisite Psalter, Lat. 10525 in the Bibliothèque Nationale at Paris; of the companion Psalter in the Fitzwilliam Museum, executed apparently for his sister Isabelle; or of the two splendid Gospel Lectionaries of the Sainte Chapelle, Lat. 8892 and 17326 in the Bibliothèque Nationale, and the somewhat later Gospel Lectionary, Add. MS. 17341 in the British Museum, also executed for the Sainte Chapelle and closely related to the second of the two Paris volumes. I shall refer to the British Museum manuscript again. Nor can we overlook the magnificent series of Old Testament Illustrations, now, except for a few detached leaves, in the Pierpont Morgan Library, New York, which must be said to reach the high-water-mark of thirteenth century illumination. St. Louis died in 1270, but the great tradition went on under his successors, of whom only two come within our period. For the first of these, Philippe III, 'le Hardi' (1270–1285), an extremely dull treatise on the Virtues and Vices was compiled in 1279 by his chaplain and confessor, Frère Laurent, or Lorens, and is known as *La Somme le Roy*. It possesses one merit, however, in that a series of fifteen pictures was designed for it, and at least two finely illuminated copies of the work have survived, both of the end of the thirteenth century. One of these is in the British Museum; of the other I shall have more to say in due course.

Of his successor, Philippe IV, 'le Bel' (1285–1314), it need only be said that in the year 1296 a Breviary was executed for him and payments were made on his behalf to an illuminator named Honoré.

§ 2. Honoré and his Atelier

The illuminator and miniaturist Honoré was no exception to the rule of anonymity, and no signed work of his is known to exist. His name is first found in a note, only partially recover-able, at the end of a splendid manuscript of the Decretals of Gratian, now MS. 558 in the Library of Tours, which tells us that the volume in question was bought in the year 1288 from Honoré the illuminator, living in Paris in the Rue Erembourc-de-Brie, now Boutebrie, for the sum of forty Paris livres. He next occurs in a Poll Tax Register of 1292, known as the Livre de la Taille, which shows him as living in this same street, the Rue Boutebrie, at that time the chief residential quarter of the lay illuminators of Paris. Sir Sydney Cockerell has incidentally reminded me that the next street to this was named the Rue des Écrivains, a clear proof of the importance attached by this date to lay craftsmen. In this Register, Honoré is shown as paying a tax of ten sous, as against eight sous paid by his son-in-law, Richard of Verdun, and two sous paid by his valet, Thomassin. The tax paid by him was higher than any paid by the other illuminators named in the Register, and the fact that he had asso-ciates working with him has been thought to prove that he must have been the head of an atelier. An entry of the following year, 1293, shows that he owned the house in which he lived, paying a rent of one denier for it. Lastly, and as a further indication of his importance, we find his name in some Royal accounts of the year 1296, which include the entry 'Honoré the illuminator, for the illumination of the King's books, 20 Livres', immediately following a note of the payment of 107 livres 10 sous for a Breviary executed for the King. He would seem to have been dead by the year 1318, as some accounts of the Sainte Chapelle for that year show his son-in-law, Richard of Verdun, as the apparent head of the atelier and in partnership with one Jean de la Mare, and they are recorded as having been paid ten livres and thirteen sous for the illumination of three large Antiphoners, which were bound by Nicholas the bookbinder. The information given above has been summarized from the pub-lished works of the great French scholars Léopold Delisle and Henry Martin. Nothing more is known at present of Honoré as an individual.

Until 1902 no extant manuscript had been associated with his name, for, although fully described in the Catalogue of the Tours Library, the Gratian had somehow escaped notice. In that year, however, Léopold Delisle issued one of his most important works, under the title *Notice de Douze Livres Royaux*, quoting in it the entry in the Royal Accounts of 1296 of the payment of 107 livres and 10 sous for a Breviary for the King, and he made the suggestion that a fine Breviary, Lat. 1023 in the Bibliothèque Nationale, could well be the actual Breviary concerned. There was evidence, as he showed, that this manuscript had been executed before 1297; it was also not only sumptuous enough to be worthy of a Royal owner, but was actually to be found in an inventory of the possessions of Charles V made in 1380. Besides a number of finely executed historiated initials this Breviary contains a magnificent full-page miniature as a frontispiece (Plate II), which, as will be seen, is in a highly distinctive style, and Delisle proceeded to suggest that this miniature was the work of Honoré's own hand. This attribution has been very generally accepted, and it is on this very beautiful miniature that Honoré's fame as a great artist may be said to have rested. A few dissentients, notably de Mély and the Abbé Leroquais, have questioned it on the ground that the miniatures in the Tours Gratian, the only manuscript to contain Honoré's name, were plainly not by the artist of the Breviary frontis-piece. Both these writers, however, failed to notice that the first miniature in the Gratian (Plate 1) is by a different hand from that or those of the other thirty-seven, and it seemed clear to me even from a very indifferent reproduction in de Mély's *Les Miniaturistes*, that this minia-ture did in fact show a rather striking resemblance to the frontispiece of the Breviary. This was more than confirmed by a visit to Paris in 1951, when the Tours Librarian, M. Georges Collon, was kind enough to bring the Gratian to the Bibliothèque Nationale, where he and I were able to compare it closely with the Breviary, and I have personally little doubt that this miniature, and in fact the decoration of the whole page, is by Honoré himself. The head of an atelier must often have confined his own share in a volume of this kind to the opening page; I think especially in this connection of another copy of the Decretals, formerly in the Yates Thompson collection, the much damaged first page of which is also almost certainly by Honoré's own hand. Fortunately this splendid Tours volume has suffered no damage and is in a perfect state of preservation; unlike so many of these large volumes of Canon Law, which were written in Italy and illuminated in the countries to which they were exported, it is an entirely French production and must surely be the finest example of this class of book in existence.

In 1906 Sir Sydney Cockerell published an article on Honoré in the December number of the *Burlington Magazine*, attributing to him a detached miniature in the Fitzwilliam Museum which had been cut from an otherwise unknown copy of *La Somme le Roy*, the treatise on the Virtues and Vices to which I have already referred. He expressed the view that it was 'mani-festly' by Honoré's own hand if the frontispiece of the Paris Breviary was correctly attributed to him, adding the words 'the book of which it is a fragment must have been a singularly beautiful one, and I do not despair of its being found at some future date'. These words were to acquire a special significance for myself many years later, little as I could have imagined it when I first read them in 1913 or thereabouts. Nothing further occurred until 1934, when Sir Sydney himself found a second leaf 'from the same splendid manuscript' in the hands of a continental bookseller and acquired it for the Fitzwilliam Museum. Four more years passed, and then, on a memorable day in 1938, the late Col. Denys Prideaux-Brune appeared in the Department of Prints and Drawings of the British Museum with some recently inherited drawings and manuscripts which he wished to deposit for safe custody, and I was asked on the telephone to come across to that Department and look at the manuscripts to save him a further journey. I did so, expecting to find the usual run of 'shop' copies of Books of Hours, as indeed were the five or so other manuscripts in the parcel, but the first one that I took out was something different, and a single glance was enough to show that I had a work of Honoré in my hands. It did not take much research to show that this was indeed the actual copy of *La*

Somme le Roy to which the two Fitzwilliam Museum miniatures belonged, with eleven minia-tures out of the original total of fifteen still in the volume. Sir Sydney Cockerell's prediction had come true after thirty-two years, and I had the satisfaction of telling him so. The study and col-lecting of medieval manuscripts has its thrills, but I do not personally expect to feel a greater one. This precious volume had been in Col. Prideaux-Brune's family since 1720, without any particular importance being attached to it, and it had only recently been valued for Probate at a fantastically low figure, which it had never occurred to him to question until I was able to undeceive him; it is an astonishing example of the way in which unsuspected treasures are still to be found in country houses even at so late a stage. The volume remained on deposit in the Department of Manuscripts for nine years, in the course of which it was removed with the rest of the collections to a place of safety during the war of 1939. Then, in 1947, a few months before my retirement, I made a suggestion to its owner, and he very generously allowed me to acquire the manuscript for my own small collection, at a figure admitted by both of us to be considerably less than its market value, on the definite understanding that it is to pass ultimately to the British Museum. His letter of 19 May of that year, written in my presence in the bedroom of a London hotel in place of a formal acknowledgment of my cheque, ends with the words 'I hope you will have many years in which to appreciate it, and that one day it will find its way to the British Museum, where I think we both feel it should eventually repose'. I pass the hotel in question almost daily, and never without thinking of that most happy transaction and recalling with gratitude the part played in it by Col. Prideaux-Brune himself, for it is not every owner of a great treasure who reacts in this fashion on being told of its importance, and the object concerned is more apt to find its way into the sale-room. Only five years later I saw with regret the announcement of his sudden death in America on 4 June 1952. Six pages of this manuscript are reproduced here (Plates 3–8); a detailed description, with reproduc-tions of all the miniatures, including the two at Cambridge, was issued by the Roxburghe Club in 1953 in a limited edition. A sister book to it is another copy of *La Somme le Roy* in the Mazarine Library, Paris (MS. 870, formerly 809), containing almost identical composi-tions. None of the miniatures are by Honoré himself, but it is obviously a product of his atelier, and was recognized as such by Sir Sydney Cockerell in his article of 1906 in the *Burlington Magazine*; it is worth noting that Sir Sydney had previously identified a detached miniature in the Cluny Museum as belonging to this volume, to which it was eventually restored. A curious point about this manuscript is that it contains a colophon with the name of the scribe, Estienne de Montbeliart, and the date 1295, while the copy that was clearly the work of the master instead of an associate contains no such information; it is, however, reason-able to suppose that it also was executed not later than 1295.

We must now consider such other manuscripts as may be attributed to Honoré or his atelier. First and foremost among these I would place a very beautiful book of Hours at Nuremberg (Stadtbibliothek, Solger in 4to, No. 4), which was executed in the first instance for English use, apparently for Canterbury. It was noted, however, by Sir Sydney Cockerell as long ago as 1900, two years before Honoré's name was coupled with any extant manuscript, as containing miniatures of the Paris school, related in style to the Yates Thompson Gratian, mentioned above as having a damaged first page almost certainly by Honoré, and I have little doubt that most if not all of the nineteen pictured pages are by Honoré himself. I have already referred to the fine Gospel Lectionary of the Sainte Chapelle, Add. MS. 17341 in the British Museum, in connection with a slightly earlier volume at Paris. The style of the British Museum volume proclaims the Honoré atelier beyond a doubt, and I would go further and suggest that the best of the initials containing miniatures are by his own hand; I think particularly of ff. 1–12 vo., which include pictures of the Entry into Jerusalem; the Annunciation; the Tree of Jesse; the Nativity and the Angel and the Shepherds; Joseph, Mary, Simeon and Anna; the Circumcision; and the Angel warning Joseph and the Flight into Egypt. Other manuscripts from the atelier must certainly include two volumes of French poetry at Paris (Bibliothèque Nationale, Franç. 12467, and Bibliothèque de l'Arsenal, MS. 3142). To the Yates Thompson Gratian I would add another at Copenhagen (Thott 160. 2⁰); a fragment of two leaves from a third Gratian, formerly in Sir Sydney Cockerell's collection and now in that of Mr. B. S. Cron; a St. Augustine, 'De Civitate Dei', formerly No. 68 in the Chester Beatty collection and now at Harvard; and a Justinian, formerly No. 67 in the same collection and now in that of Major J. R. Abbey, although all the work in this last would seem to be by an associate. Other manuscripts will no doubt be assigned to the atelier or even to Honoré himself as his style becomes better known.

A few words should perhaps be said in conclusion about Honoré's style, although it is only from the plates in this volume that any real idea of it can be obtained, and no description can really help towards its recognition. The most that I can do here is to draw attention to what I think are some of this great artist's characteristics as they are found in the eight pages reproduced in this publication. I would give the first place to his very marked facial types, especially those with beards, as for example Samuel and Jesse in Plate 2 and the left hand Apostle and St. Peter in Plate 3. The beards are either pincer-shaped or long and straggling, both kinds appearing in Plate 3. The hair is curly and finely drawn, in brown, grey, or grey blue, a curious feature being a small patch of hair in the middle of the forehead where the head itself is bald (see three of the figures in Plate 3, and Jonathan in Plate 7); there are also, sometimes, small dots on the bald scalps representing hair, as in the case of St. Peter in Plate 3. The faces in general show a greater modelling than is usual even so late in the thirteenth century, while there is a very real characterisation in some cases, notably the sinner and the jeering hypocrite in Plate 6, the contrite expression of the former being especially remarkable. The eyebrows are arched, in some cases almost taking the shape of an inverted V, a point that is well illustrated in Plate 3.

The backgrounds are normally either burnished gold with a delicate branching pattern in matt gold (see Plate 2, *upper compartment*, Plates 3–5, Plate 6, *upper right and lower left compartments*, Plate 7, *upper left and lower right compartments*, Plate 8; there is an occasional variant, as in Plate 7, where the backgrounds of the other two compartments are light red), or a lozenge diaper, which in the pages reproduced is alternately burnished gold, and blue with matt gold fleurs de lis (see Plate 2, *lower compartment*, and Plate 6, *upper left and lower right compartments*). The names of the persons or personifications (Plates 2, 5–8) or the subjects of the miniatures (Plates 3, 4) are shown above or below, chiefly in the margins. The frames, as Sir Sydney Cockerell has noted, have a very delicate pattern in white on a blue or pink ground, with gold quatrefoils at the corners, 'somewhat in the manner of an Oxford frame', a perfect description in 1906, although one may perhaps wonder how far such a frame is known nowadays. All the Plates except Plate 4 show this feature.

But when all is said and done, it is the eye alone and its familiarity with the originals and with the best available reproductions that will enable us to identify any further works of Honoré or his atelier yet to be discovered.

As has already been suggested, Honoré himself was almost certainly dead by 1318, although his atelier continued to flourish. The three large Antiphoners of the Sainte Chapelle for which his son-in-law Richard of Verdun and the latter's partner Jean de la Mare received payment in that year have long since disappeared, or at least have not been identified. Nor does it now seem possible to distinguish the atelier in its later period, although it is beyond dispute that Honoré's style continued to influence his successors, and that, too, well into the fourteenth century. This influence is clearly visible in such manuscripts as the Life of St. Denis in three volumes, Franç. 2090–2 in the Bibliothèque Nationale, with its delightful pictures of medieval Paris, which was given to Philippe le Long by the abbot of Saint Denis in 1317. It is to be seen still more clearly in the work of his great fourteenth-century successor, Jean Pucelle, the discovery of whose name, in a Bible dated 1327 and in the now well-known Belleville Breviary, by Léopold Delisle, was another landmark in the history of French illumination. In the Breviary in particular, Lat. 10483–4 in the Bibliothèque Nationale, the bearded facial types are almost exactly repeated, as are other of Honoré's characteristics, and one would dearly like to know whether Pucelle himself could have received his early training in Honoré's atelier. Some document that will throw light on the matter is perhaps still awaiting discovery, but in the meantime it is unwise to speculate any further.

Note. Readers wishing to verify any statements made above will find references in the following work, especially in the footnotes to pp. 2–6: '*An Illuminated Manuscript of La Somme le Roy, Attributed to the Parisian Miniaturist Honoré*, with Introduction by Eric George Millar, D.Litt., F.S.A., Oxford, Printed for the Roxburghe Club, 1953', a copy of which is in the British Museum Library.

PLATE 1

GRATIAN, DECRETALS

Late XIII Century (before A.D. 1288)
Tours, Bibliothèque Municipale, MS. 558, f. 1 (*portion only, reduced*)
(Size of full page, 460 × 290 mm.)

The only manuscript containing Honoré's name, which occurs in a note in Latin at the end of the volume, beginning: 'In the year of our Lord twelve hundred and eighty eight I bought the present Decretals from Honoré the illuminator dwelling at Paris in the street Herenenboc de Bria (now Rue Boutebrie) for the sum of forty Paris livres. . . .' The Plate shows the first miniature in the volume, which is almost certainly by Honoré's own hand; a king is dictating the law to a scribe, a group of six persons, including a knight, a clerk, and a civil judge, standing behind on the right.

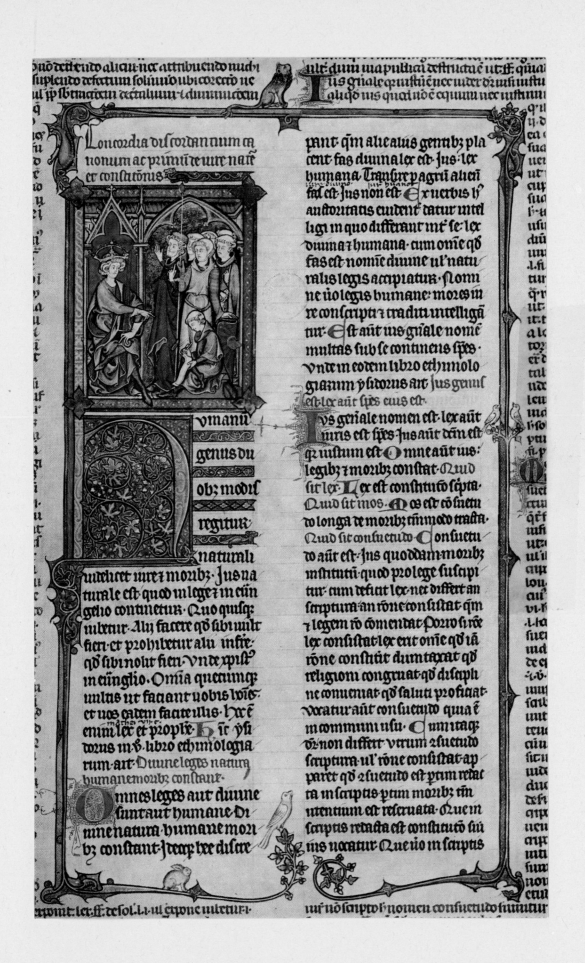

Concordia discordantium ca-
nonum ac primum de iure nat-
ure et constitutionis.

Humanum
genus du-
obus modis
regitur,
naturali
videlicet iure et moribus. Ius na-
turale est quod in lege et evangelio continetur. Quo quisque
iubetur alii facere quod sibi uult
fieri et prohibetur alii inferre
quod sibi nolit fieri. Vnde christus
in evangelio. Omnia quecunque
uultis ut faciant uobis homines
et uos eadem facite illis. Hec e-
nim lex et prophete. Sic isi-
dorus in .v. libro ethimologia-
rum ait. Diuine leges natura
humane moribus constant.

Omnes leges aut diuine
sunt aut humane. Di-
uine natura humane mori-
bus constant; ideoque hee discre-
pant quoniam alie aliis genti-
bus placent, fas diuina lex est; ius lex
humana. Transire per agrum alie-
num fas est; ius non est. Ex verbis hu-
ius auctoritatis euidenter datur intel-
ligi in quo differant inter se lex
diuina et humana, cum omne quod
fas est nomine diuine uel natu-
ralis legis accipiatur, si nomine uero legis humane, mores in
re conscripti et traditi intelligan-
tur. Est autem ius generale nomen
multas sub se continens species.
Vnde in eodem libro ethimolo-
giarum ysidorus ait. Ius generale
est, lex autem species eius est.

Ius generale nomen est, lex autem
iuris est species. Ius autem dictum est
quia iustum est. Omne autem ius
legibus et moribus constat. Quid
sit lex. Lex est constitutio scripta.
Quid sit mos. Mos est consuetudo longa de moribus tantummodo tracta.
Quid sit consuetudo. Consuetudo autem est ius quoddam moribus
institutum quod pro lege suscipi-
tur cum deficit lex; nec differt an
scriptura an ratione consistat quoniam
et legem ratio commendat. Porro si ratione
lex consistat, lex erit omne quod ratione consistit dumtaxat quod
religioni congruat, quod discipli-
ne conueniat, quod saluti proficiat.
Vocatur autem consuetudo quia est
in communi usu. Cum itaque
dictum est non differt utrum consuetudo
scriptura uel ratione consistat ap-
paret quod consuetudo est partim redacta in scriptis, partim moribus tan-
tum retentum est reseruata. Que in
scriptis redacta est constitutio siue
ius uocatur. Que uero non in scriptis

PLATE 2

BREVIARY OF PHILIPPE LE BEL

End of XIII Century (probably before A.D. 1296)
Paris, Bibliothèque Nationale, lat. 1023, f. 7 vo.
(Size of full page, 205 × 135 mm.)

The well-known frontispiece, the attribution of which to Honoré in 1902 by Léopold Delisle, on the strength of an entry in some Royal accounts of 1296, established Honoré's reputation as a great artist.

The subjects represented are: (1) *Upper compartment*. The anointing of David by Samuel, Jesse, whose name is given above as 'ysai', standing with his other sons on the right, in front of the city of Bethlehem. (2) *Lower compartment*. David slings a stone at Goliath, Saul standing on the left; on the right, David cuts off Goliath's head with the latter's sword.

LA SOMME LE ROY

End of XIII Century (probably before A.D. 1295)
London, Collection of Dr. E. G. Millar
(The reproductions are actual size, but the margins have been trimmed)

The Treatise on the Virtues and Vices compiled in 1279 by the Dominican Frère Laurent or Lorens for Philippe III, le Hardi, King of France, to whom he was confessor. It consists of a series of moral treatises on the Commandments, the Creed, the seven deadly sins, etc. A cycle of fifteen pictures was compiled for it, whether by the author himself or by some other hand is not certain, no illustrated copies being in existence earlier than the end of the thir-teenth century. The present manuscript, which came to light in 1938, contains eleven out of the total of fifteen pictures; two others are in the Fitzwilliam Museum, Cambridge, and the remaining two have still to be discovered. All thirteen miniatures are ascribed to Honoré.

PLATE III

La Somme le Roy, f. 10 vo.

The Apostles composing the Creed, St. Peter in the centre pointing to its opening words, which he holds on a lectern. The text assigns each article of the Creed to a different Apostle the first being given to St. Peter.

Côment li apostre font la credo.

reproduction suffers from anaemia. Red colours marked - definite shading.
Main colours bright blue — blue-grey, and orange.
Top peach colour. A faded vermillion, with gold scrolly, is close.
Writing nearer vermillion.

PLATE 4

La Somme le Roy, f. 69 vo.

The Seven Virgins watering the trees of the mystic garden. The description in French below may be translated as follows:

'This is the garden of the Virtues. The seven trees signify the seven Virtues of which this book speaks. The tree in the centre signifies Jesus Christ under whom the Virtues grow. The seven springs of this garden are the seven gifts of the Holy Spirit which water the garden. The seven maidens who draw water from these seven springs are the seven petitions of the Pater Noster which pray for the seven gifts of the Holy Spirit.'

At the bottom of the picture is a hunting scene, very delicately drawn, in which a huntsman and two hounds chase a stag to the right, while a lion with a long tail moves in the opposite direction, having no apparent interest in the hunt.

Cell li iardins des vinz. Il og. arbre senefient les vy. vinz dont
eist liurs parle. Li. arbre du melieu senefie ihuerist. souz q
cwissent les vinz. Les vy. fontaines de cest iardin sont les vy
dons du saint espent qui arousent le iardin. Les vy. pucelles
qui puisent en ces vy. fontaines sont les vy. peticions de
la patrnostre qui emprient les vy. dons du saint espent...

PLATE 5

La Somme le Roy, f. 91 vo.

Miniature in four compartments, with personifications of the four Virtues, Prudence, Temperance, Fortitude, and Justice, all represented as crowned female figures. (1) *Upper left compartment.* Prudence, seated on the left at a lectern, on which is an open book, instructs three seated maidens, two of whom hold books. Her name 'prudence' is in red in the upper margin. (2) *Upper right compartment.* Temperance, standing behind a table on which a meal is spread, admonishing a girl on the right who appears to be declining a cup offered her by a kneeling man. Her name, 'attrempance' is in black in the upper margin. (3) *Lower left compartment.* Fortitude stands on a river, holding a medallion on which is a lion. (The river is probably intended for the Tigris, to which this virtue was compared by St. Ambrose.) Her name, 'force' is in black in the lower margin. (4) *Lower right compartment.* Justice is seated on a throne, holding the scales in her right hand and a sword in her left. Her name, 'Justice' is in red in the lower margin.

PLATE 6

La Somme le Roy, f. 97 vo.

Miniature in four compartments, showing the personification of the Virtue of Humility, an example of this Virtue, and two examples of the contrasting Vices, Pride and Hypocrisy. (1) *Upper left compartment.* Humility, represented as a crowned female figure, stands on a unicorn and holds in her right hand a white wand and in her left a medallion on which is a standing woman also holding a white wand. Her name, 'humilite' is in red in the upper margin. (2) *Upper right compartment.* Ahaziah, typifying Pride, falls headlong from the tower of a castellated building. The name of the Vice, 'orgueil' and his name 'occozias' are in black and red respectively in the upper margin. (3) *Lower left compartment.* The sinner kneels facing an altar on the right, on which is a golden chalice under a silver tabernacle. His contrite expression and general attitude show remarkable characterisation on the part of the artist. His description, 'le pecheeur' is in red in the lower margin. (4) *Lower right compartment.* The hypocrite, kneeling at a bare altar, looks round to the left and points derisively at the sinner. His description, 'lypocrite' is in red in the lower margin.

humilite · orgueil · occozias ·

le pecheeur · ypocrite ·

PLATE 7

La Somme le Roy, f. 107

Miniature in four compartments showing personifications of the Virtue of Friendship and the Vice of Hatred, with an example of each. (1) *Upper left compartment.* Friendship, a crowned female figure, stands on a dragon and holds a medallion on which is a dove. Her name, 'Amistie' is in red in the upper margin. (2) *Upper right compartment.* Hatred, a standing bearded man, in an attitude suggesting anger or despair. His name, 'hely' is in black in the upper margin, a word which has not yet been explained, and is probably a mistake for 'haine', which is found in the miniature of this subject in the fine manuscript of La Somme le Roy of the same date, in the British Museum, Add. MS. 28162, f. 6 vo. (3) *Lower left compartment.* David and Jonathan embrace one another, typifying friendship, Jonathan being represented as an elderly bearded man for some reason. Their names are written in black in the lower margin. (4) *Lower right compartment.* Saul threatens David's life with an arrow in place of the usual javelin; David is seated on the left, with harp. This subject is typical of Hatred. Their names are in red in the lower margin.

Amistie   hely

Dauid etJonathas   saul. et Dauid.

Green is quite good but should be strong, blues more grey.

PLATE 8

La Somme le Roy, 1. 136 vo.

Miniature in four compartments, showing a personification and example of the Virtue of Mercy, with examples of the Vice of Avarice and of its contrasting Virtue. (1) *Upper left compartment.* Mercy, a crowned female figure, holding a medallion on which are a hen and chickens, puts a garment over the head of a man stripped to the waist. She is standing on a wolf which seizes a lamb between the man's legs. Her name, 'misericorde' is in black in the upper margin. (2) *Upper right compartment.* Avarice, a bearded and ragged miser, transfers some gold coins from a small chest into a larger closed one through an opening in the side with hinged door. He is being advised and encouraged by a devil seated on the lid of the larger chest. The name, 'auarice' is in red in the upper margin. (3) *Lower left compartment.* Lot receives the two angels, who are dressed as pilgrims but show their wings. (In the corresponding miniature of the Somme le Roy in the British Museum, Add. MS. 28162, f. 9 vo., Abraham is shown instead, receiving the three angels.) The words 'loth qui recoit les angels' are in red in the lower margin. (4) *Lower right compartment.* The widow and her oil (2 Kings, iv. 1–7). The words 'la bonne fame qui depart luile' are in black in the lower margin.